June '14

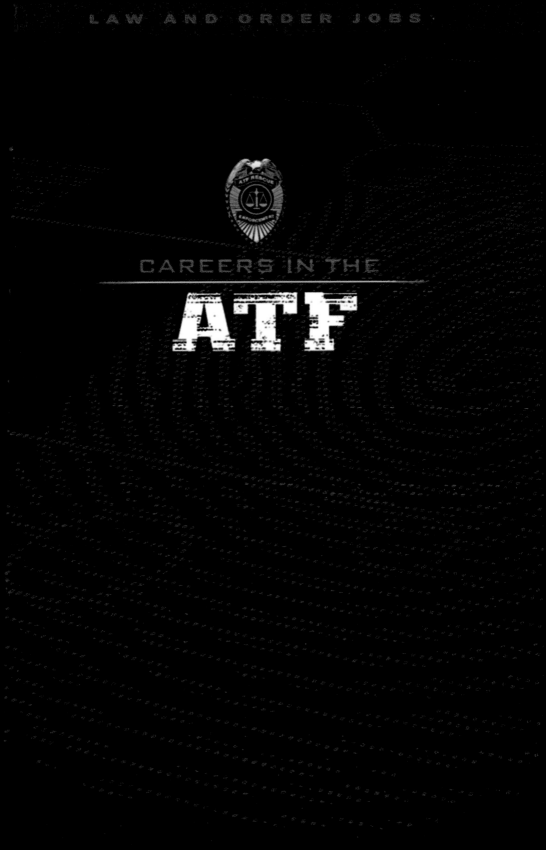

CAREERS IN THE

ATF

CAREERS IN THE
ATF

BY ADAM WOOG

Cavendish
Square

New York

Once again, this one's for Leah.

Published in 2014 by Cavendish Square Publishing, LLC
303 Park Avenue South, Suite 1247, New York, NY 10010

Copyright © 2014 by Cavendish Square Publishing, LLC

First Edition

CPSIA Compliance Information: Batch #WW14CSQ

All websites were available and accurate when this book was sent to press.

LIBRARY OF CONGRESS CATALOGING-IN-PUBLICATION DATA
Woog, Adam, 1953-
Careers in the ATF / Adam Woog.
p. cm. — (Law and order jobs)
Includes bibliographical references and index.
ISBN 978-1-62712-428-7 (hardcover) ISBN 978-1-62712-429-4 (paperback) ISBN 978-1-62712-430-0 (ebook)
1. United States. Bureau of Alcohol, Tobacco, and Firearms—Vocational guidance—Juvenile literature.
2. Criminal investigation—Vocational guidance—United States—Juvenile literature. 3. Law enforcement—
Vocational guidance—United States—Juvenile literature. I. Title. HV8144.B87W66 2014 363.28—dc23
2011045888

ART DIRECTOR: Anahid Hamparian   SERIES DESIGNER: Michael Nelson
LAYOUT DESIGN: Joseph Macri   EDITOR: Dean Miller
Photo research by Marybeth Kavanaugh

The photographs in this book are used by permission and through the courtesy of: Cover photo by AP Photo/John Amis. *Getty:* Marvin Joseph/*Washington Post*, 2-3; Alex Wong, 18; *AP Photo*: Chris Vinn/Tyler Morning Telegraph, 7; David Longstreath, 14; Kiichiro Sato, 27; Michael Green, 30; John Amis, 55; Alan Diaz, 69; Janet S. Carter/*The Free Press*, 73; *Everett Collection*: 22; *The Art Archive*: Gunshots, 20; *Landov*: Jeff Topping/Reuters, 33; *Newscom*: J. Emilio Flores/La Opinion, 38; ZUMA Press, 60; HO/AFP/Getty Images, 77; *PhotoEdit Inc.*: A. Ramey, 50; *Alamy*: Reportage/Archival Image, 66; *ATF*: covers (seal).

Printed in the United States of America

CONTENTS

THE ATF IN ACTION

IT STARTED ON NEW YEAR'S DAY, 2010.

Bill Parr, the pastor of Little Hope Baptist Church near Canton, Texas, was reading the newspaper when the phone rang. Canton is a small East Texas town, about 55 miles (88.5 km) from Dallas. The caller told Parr that smoke was issuing from the church. The pastor called 911 and learned that fire units were already on their way. But they arrived too late to save a good portion of the church. The fire destroyed or badly damaged areas such as its education space, fellowship hall, and kitchen.

The Little Hope church was just the beginning.

Within hours, another church fire broke out. This one was on the outskirts of Athens, Texas, about 25 miles (40 km) from Canton. Once again local firefighters responded, and once again there was major damage.

Two weeks later, two more churches burned on the same night: Grace Community Church and Lake Athens Baptist Church, both near Athens. Both churches were severely damaged, in part because the simultaneous fires stretched local firefighting resources thin.

Firefighters respond to a blaze at the Dover Baptist Church in Smith County, Texas. This was the latest in a rash of such fires. When investigators couldn't get to the root of it, they called in the ATF.

At the Lake Athens site, investigators found two clues: a Skechers shoe print and a Red Wing boot print, indicating that there were at least two offenders. Investigators also recovered a piece of concrete that had been thrown through a window to provide a way in. Furthermore, they found the source of the blaze: books, wooden chairs, and other **flammable** materials had been stacked around the sanctuary and set on fire.

The clear conclusion: the fires were **arson**.

The destruction didn't stop with those four churches. On January 16, a fire at Tyland Baptist Church in Tyler, Texas, heavily damaged that structure. The next day, a fifth East Texas church went up in flames: First Church of Christ Science, also in Tyler. And three days later, there was still another blaze, this time at Prairie Creek Fellowship Church in Lindale.

The residents of East Texas were terrified. There were no deaths, but property damage was in the millions, and the possibility of injury or loss of life was very real. By this time, hundreds of volunteers were patrolling churches and looking for suspicious activity.

Although there seemed to be no pattern that would explain *why* the blazes were being set, there were similarities in *how* they were set. For example, with one exception, the arsonists broke a window to get in. Also, the offenders always started a fire by igniting books, chairs, and other flammable items that they'd stacked in a central location.

However, there were also many differences between these fires and typical serial arsons. For example, they took place at different times of both day and night; most serial arson cases occur at night. Additionally, serial arsons often take place in a concentrated area, such as a specific neighborhood. In this case, fires were being set across a huge area—about 2,600 square miles (4184 sq km) in three counties. Furthermore, most arsonists work alone, but in the East Texas series, at least two people were working together.

These arsons did not appear to be racially motivated or limited to any one Christian denomination. In fact, statistics show that in general there is no single motivation for church arsons. Alabama State Fire Marshal Ed Paulk, who was a lead investigator in a string of church arsons in that state in 2006, commented,

> [Investigators] try to keep an open mind and allow evidence to steer where we go and what we look at . . . whereas the public tends to sensationalize what they perceive to be motive. . . . We've had situations where the motivation was covering up burglaries and theft, [or] where it was acting out against people in revenge, and we've had cases where it had to do with

the occult, and cases where people are just making poor judgments.

No matter what the motivations are, church fires are generally considered particularly awful. They are seen as a strike against the fundamental idea of religious faith. This was perhaps especially true in deeply religious East Texas. Randy Daniels, the mayor of Athens, told CNN, "I think maybe I would characterize the mood of our people as perplexed. . . . I think most people would just wonder who could be doing this or even why. Most people consider it just incomprehensible and unconscionable that somebody could and would be doing this."

THE INVESTIGATION

After the first few fires, local authorities were overwhelmed. They simply did not have the resources to do a thorough investigation. They asked for help from the federal government, and it came from the U.S. Bureau of Alcohol, Tobacco, Firearms, and Explosives (ATF).

To handle the situation, the ATF agents and arson specialists, along with local law enforcement authorities, formed a task force; its headquarters were in an old National Guard armory in Athens. The team included more than seventy ATF agents, thirty Texas Rangers, forty Texas Department of Public Safety criminal investigators, and troopers, fire marshals, and police and sheriff departments from three counties. About thirty of them belonged to ATF's National Response Team (NRT). The NRT consists of highly trained specialists who focus on the aftermath of major fires and explosions.

The East Texas Arson Task Force, as the joint venture was called, began analyzing evidence and interviewing eyewitnesses. The ATF also posted a $10,000 reward for information leading to the arrest of the criminals.

For about two weeks there were no more incidents. Then, early on the morning of February 4, the historic Russell Memorial United Methodist Church in Wills Point was set ablaze with the same telltale methods. This was an especially brazen crime—the church was across the street from the Wills Point Volunteer Fire Department. Clay Alexander, an ATF special agent who was part of the task force, recalled, "Talk about bold. I mean they even broke into the church on the side of the building closest to the fire department. It was like they were playing with us."

Four days later, there were two more incidents: Dover Baptist Church in Tyler and Clear Spring Missionary Baptist Church in Lindale were set ablaze. Skechers shoe prints were found at the Tyler church that matched the one found in Lake Athens.

By this time, the case was shaping up to be one of the longest strings of arsons seen by the ATF. Franceska Perot, a public information officer for the bureau, commented to a reporter for East Texas television station KLTV, "There have been serial arsons in the past, but this is fast approaching one of the largest ones that we have ever worked on."

Then investigators received a major break in the case. Jason Robert Bourque, age nineteen, and Daniel George McAllister, twenty-one, were caught on video at two convenience stores near the two most recent fires, shortly after the blazes had been reported. The task force now had major persons of interest and things began to move quickly.

The ATF raised the reward money to $25,000 and an insurance company added another $30,000. Within days, a phone call—one of hundreds of tips that had come in—further focused attention on Bourque and McAllister. (It was later revealed that the call came from the wife of a friend of theirs.)

On February 11, ATF agents visited Bourque's grandparents' home, where the young suspect was living. They were looking for a blue Ford Focus that had been seen near the fires, a car model that Bourque drove. When they asked to see his car, agents spotted a pair of muddy Skechers. They already knew that McAllister, the other suspect, sometimes wore a type of Red Wing boot that matched the boot print they had recovered earlier.

The agents didn't mention anything about footwear to Bourque. Instead, they began a surveillance operation and noticed that he was acting strangely. Davis recalls, "He just did some things that made it seem like he knew he was being watched. But the big thing was that he was driving by some of the fire scenes on his way from [a junior college where he was a student] to his home, and these were not routes one would typically take."

THE ARRESTS

Two days later, on February 13, agents followed Bourque to Atwoods, a farm and hardware store. After he left, store employees found a message carved in the restroom: "Little Hope was Arson," with an upside-down cross in flames. ATF agents removed the stall wall and sent it to the bureau's main lab in Maryland for testing. Meanwhile, video footage confirmed that Bourque had used that restroom that day.

A few days later, agents were able to match his DNA. They got a sample from a cigarette butt that Bourque had discarded and matched it with evidence taken from a rock found inside the Wills Point church. This evidence was strong enough for ATF agents and the Texas Rangers to obtain search warrants. Alexander stated, "Learning the results of the DNA testing . . . was the galvanizing event for all of us to say collectively, 'These are the guys.'"

In the early morning of February 21, Judge Jack Skeen Jr. signed two arrest warrants. Within the hour, a heavily armed SWAT team surrounded the mobile home in Grand Saline where Bourque was staying. They threw flash grenades through the windows, smashed the front door, and arrested Bourque without further violence. Meanwhile, another team of law enforcement officers found and arrested McAllister at his girlfriend's home, hundreds of miles away in Seguin.

In announcing the conclusion of the East Texas church arsons, Robert Champion, ATF Special Agent in Charge in Dallas, commented, "ATF has been a proud partner in this case. We had over seventy agents, both local and members of two National Response Teams working on this investigation since the beginning. All agencies involved will continue to work together towards our goal of a successful prosecution of those involved in these crimes."

Bourque and McAllister pleaded guilty in courts in three counties. Their motives were not clear, although both indicated that they had committed the crimes because they had turned away from organized religion. Furthermore, Borque blamed his confused state of mind on his abuse of drugs, including an antismoking medication. Both were sentenced to life in prison.

The case was the 688th time that ATF's National Response Team had been called out since the program began in 1978. But ATF does far more than send emergency teams to crisis situations.

Rescue workers look on at the devastation caused when the Alfred P. Murrah Federal building was bombed by Timothy McVeigh on April 19, 1995.

THE
BIG PICTURE

THE NAME PRETTY MUCH SAYS IT ALL. THE BUREAU of Alcohol, Tobacco, Firearms and Explosives is the U.S. government agency that enforces federal laws relating to . . . well, alcohol, tobacco, firearms, and explosives.

More specifically, the ATF is part of the U.S. Department of Justice, and its main jobs are to investigate and stop federal offenses that involve the unlawful use, manufacture, or possession of firearms or explosives; the smuggling and illegal manufacture or sale of tobacco and alcohol products; and acts of arson and bombings. The ATF also oversees the regulation and licensing of companies and people involved in the sale, possession, and transportation of firearms, ammunition, and explosives.

When necessary, the ATF identifies and apprehends suspected criminals and turns them over to the proper authorities. But much of its work involves overseeing and regulating legitimate organizations and companies. For example, the explosive used in the deadly Oklahoma City bombing in 1995 contained ammonium nitrate, a chemical often used in agriculture. In the wake of the explosion, the ATF worked with the agriculture industry to create a program making it easier for fertilizer-manufacturing companies to report thefts of the chemical. As the ATF's website notes,

> While ATF is primarily concerned with law enforcement and regulatory duties, we also strive to work and consult with the industries we regulate and the businesses, agencies, and groups that affect them. By doing this, we hope to develop more efficient, more effective, and less burdensome programs, policies, and procedures.

The bureau's widely varied set of duties may seem unconnected. In part, that's true. Alcohol and tobacco logically go together, as do explosives and firearms. But what connects the two pairs? An article on a website maintained by the Transactional Records Access Clearinghouse at Syracuse University states, "As suggested by its name, and unlike the Internal Revenue Service and the Drug Enforcement Agency, the Bureau of Alcohol, Tobacco, Firearms and Explosives (ATF) has over the years been assigned a variety of responsibilities that were not always obviously connected."

In some ways, the reason behind this disconnect is just a series of historical flukes. These flukes happened as the agency evolved and took on different tasks. Today, the abbreviation ATF has been retained, even though the bureau's job also includes explosive-related issues. Furthermore, its role in regulating alcohol and tobacco taxes is not as important as it once was. So the name is not completely accurate, and this can lead to confusion. Mark D. Jones, who has served as the head of the ATF's Arson and Explosives Intelligence Branch, remarks that if the abbreviation changed, "It would make explaining what I do a little bit easier."

WHAT THE ATF DOES

The ATF's job is a big one. However, the bureau is relatively small in comparison to other federal law enforcement agencies. At the end of 2010, it had about 5,000 employees; the FBI, on the other hand, had roughly 35,700. Many of the ATF's employees are stationed at the bureau's headquarters in Washington, D.C., while others work in offices, labs, and other facilities around the country.

Of the bureau's employees, the most familiar to the public are special agents. These armed officers primarily carry out investigations of federal crimes involving explosives, arson, and/or firearms.

In most cases, the ATF is the lead federal agency in investigating bombings within the United States. In cases of bombings related to international terrorism or civil rights, however, the FBI serves as the lead agency. The two agencies' responsibilities often overlap, but the ATF's role tends to be more similar to that of patrol police officers. One ATF agent commented, "We fashion ourselves as federal street cops, and [the FBI's] job is to see a bigger picture, a global connection."

Another major component of the ATF is its team of investigators. Investigators are not armed, and despite their

Debris of a pipe bomb is displayed at the forensic special case laboratory of ATF headquarters in Maryland. The laboratory is the only one of its kind in the world.

name, they are not necessarily directly involved in criminal investigations. Their primary responsibility is to inspect and regulate the firearms and explosives industries. In other words, they make sure that laws, licensing requirements, and other regulations are properly observed. It's not the bureau's most glamorous job, but it's one of the most important—so much so that the organization calls its investigators "the backbone of the ATF regulatory mission."

Supporting the investigators, meanwhile, is a large contingent of other ATF employees. This support staff covers a wide spectrum of jobs. Some support workers are professionals, such as lawyers and information technology specialists, as well as **auditors** and **forensic** scientists. Other support staff serve as surveillance technicians, assistants, maintenance crews, and office employees.

As a whole, this workforce is busier than ever. For one thing, consider the number of active investigations. In the first years of the twenty-first century, the ATF averaged about 40 new investigations annually. As of 2011, however, the annual average of new cases for the bureau was about 130.

Furthermore, the ATF has proved to be more effective and efficient than other federal law enforcement agencies. Overall, for example, it outpaces these other agencies in the number of cases recommended for prosecution—that is, in how many offenders are apprehended and held for trial.

The numbers tell the story. In the first half of 2011, the 2,000 or so ATF special agents recommended about 5,200 cases for prosecution—an average of about 2.5 per agent. Compare this to the statistics for the FBI. During the same period, FBI special agents (about 13,000) recommended more than 8,800 cases for prosecution—averaging about 1.2 cases for the year, half that of the ATF.

Furthermore, the ATF is noted for using its annual budget effectively. In 2011, the budget was more than a billion dollars. It's estimated that ATF gives a 35-to-1 return on the dollar. In other words, for every dollar it spends, the bureau recovers $35 for the government. Simply put, the bureau gives good value for the money.

THE ATF'S LONG HISTORY

For many years, the ATF brought in revenue by acting as a collection agency for alcohol and tobacco taxes. However, as a result of changes in regulations (notably, the creation of a federal income tax), this aspect of the ATF has become less important over the years. At the same time, other facets of the organization's work have become increasingly important.

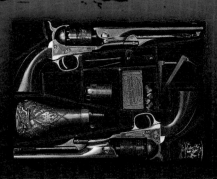

Firearms that are considered unusual, rare, or of historic significance are generally classified by ATF as "curio and relic" (C&R) weapons. Broadly speaking, to qualify as a curio or relic, a firearm must fall into at least one of three categories: it must be older than fifty years (not including replicas); it must not be intended for sporting use or as an offensive or defensive weapon; and it must be what ATF refers to as "novel, rare, bizarre, or [of interest] because of [its] association with some historical figure, period, or event."

The following passage, from a 2009 article about an auction of rare guns, gives a glimpse into the world of C&R guns, by focusing on the sale of one firearm of particular significance: a pistol once owned by the infamous bandit Jesse James.

One of the most historical firearms in this auction is the Colt 1860 Army Percussion Revolver and holster rig that at one time belonged to one of the most notorious outlaws of all times, Jesse James. It is believed that Jesse carried this gun when he was with Quantrill's Raiders and merely a teenager. Unlike most alleged Jesse James guns today, this one carries an impeccable pedigree. At the time of Jesse's death, the gun was given by his wife, together with other effects of Jesse James, to his closest and personal friends, his two cousins, who had ridden with him with Quantrill's Raiders.

The gun's holster, with a unique scarlet and engraved belt buckle, has James's scratched signature on two places. However, more importantly, within the year after Jesse's cousins were given the gun and holster rig, they had their picture taken at Winans Photography Rooms in Independence, Missouri. At that time they very proudly wore and brandished the holster rig and pistol. Accompanying the [gun and holster], which came directly from an eighty-two-year-old descendant of the original cousin who inherited the gun, is an affidavit of history along with a large compilation of paperwork, genealogy, etc.

Above: One of the most famous guns in American history is Jesse James's Colt 1860 Army Percussion Revolver.

These changes can be traced to the bureau's beginnings. Its ancestry dates to the period just after the birth of the United States, when the government needed an organization to impose taxes on alcohol. But the bureau didn't begin to take on anything like its modern form until 1886, when it became known as the Revenue Laboratory. This agency was responsible for analyzing liquor to check for purity, but it also collected taxes on alcoholic beverages. Then, in 1920, it was renamed the Alcohol Tax Unit (ATU).

This name change coincided with a dramatic period in American history: Prohibition. During this era, 1920–1933, the manufacture, sale, and distribution of alcoholic beverages was illegal in the United States. Prohibition remains the most infamous segment of the bureau's history—the wild and raucous time when Al Capone, Dutch Schultz, and other gangsters grew rich and famous by means of **bootlegging** liquor. The Alcohol Tax Unit's job was to enforce the federal bans on alcohol. On the front lines of this job were the unit's "revenuers" (or "revenoors"), including the legendary Eliot Ness.

The bureau's job description changed when Prohibition ended in the mid–1930s, and its role began to evolve again. *Los Angeles Times* reporter Scott Glover comments, "Back then, it was all about booze. Over the years, though, Congress expanded the role of the bureau. The National Firearms Act of 1934 placed restrictions on so-called gangster guns and charged the ATF with enforcing the law."

Later, in 1952, the organization changed yet again. In addition to its existing duties, it was given the task of enforcing

After President John F. Kennedy was assassinated in Dallas, Texas, on November 22, 1963, presidents never rode in open-topped cars again.

tobacco tax laws. To reflect this, the organization took a new name: the Alcohol and Tobacco Tax Division (ATTD). In the next decade, the 1960s, the assassinations by gunfire of President John F. Kennedy, his brother Robert Kennedy, and Dr. Martin Luther King Jr. led to tightened restrictions on firearms nationwide. This enhanced the organization's role as "the gun police," and in time the organization's name became the Bureau of Alcohol, Tobacco, and Firearms (ATF).

The most recent change in the bureau's duties came in 2003. In the wake of the 9/11 terrorist attacks two years before, there was a massive reshuffling of government law enforcement agencies. As part of the changes, ATF was moved from the Treasury Department to the Justice Department and renamed. Although still informally called ATF, the agency's official name today is the Bureau of Alcohol, Tobacco, Firearms, and Explosives.

During the Prohibition era (1920–1933), alcohol was illegal in the United States. The most famous figure in the fight to enforce antiliquor laws was an agent of the Treasury Department, Eliot Ness. Based in Chicago, Ness had the primary job of tracking down members of organized crime syndicates who manufactured, smuggled, and distributed banned liquor.

In particular, Ness is remembered for his ongoing battle against Al Capone, the infamous Chicago gangster who oversaw a huge criminal empire, the heart of which was liquor. Capone maintained his hold on the city's criminal activities through intimidation, which was often deadly, and by bribing corrupt politicians, policemen, and other government officials.

But Ness and the nine agents under him broke this stranglehold by eliminating Capone's main sources of income. They used surveillance, anonymous tips, wiretapping, and other methods to seize several key parts of the mobster's network of breweries and distilleries. Along the way, Ness and his men gained a reputation for being completely immune to Capone's bribery or threats—a reputation that led to a Chicago newspaper reporter dubbing them the "Untouchables."

Despite the dangers—including the murder of a close friend and threats against his parents—Ness persevered. In time, Al Capone was sentenced to eleven years in prison for tax evasion, the only charge against him for which the government had enough evidence to ensure a conviction. Ness went on to become the chief investigator of the Chicago Prohibition Bureau. After that, he spearheaded another operation: locating and destroying moonshine (homemade alcohol) operations in remote parts of Ohio, Kentucky, and Tennessee.

After Prohibition, Ness had further successes in crime enforcement. He became the lead investigator in a campaign to clean up rampant crime and police corruption in Cleveland, Ohio. He and the thirty-four agents under him gathered evidence against a large pool of corrupt police officers and city officials. When Ness's unit presented its findings to a grand jury in 1936, it resulted in more than two hundred resignations and/or convictions.

Ness also succeeded in improving the notoriously poor safety record of drivers on Cleveland's streets and highways, where an average of 250 deaths and many more injuries had been occurring every year. The lawman created a separate, citywide traffic court that focused on such issues as drunk drivers, police officers who fixed tickets, and automobiles lacking licensing and inspection papers. Within a few years, traffic deaths in the city plummeted to half of what they'd been in previous years.

ALCOHOL AND TOBACCO ENFORCEMENT

Along the way, two of the ATF's early jobs—licensing and taxing tobacco and alcohol—became the responsibility of the Treasury Department's Alcohol and Tobacco Tax and Trade Bureau (TTB). Nonetheless, the ATF is still responsible for enforcing illegal acts involving those substances.

For example, the ATF investigates cigarette smuggling. This criminal activity thrives because taxes charged on cigarettes and other tobacco products differ from state to state. Some states have almost no tax; others charge several dollars per pack. As a result, organized crime has long been involved in large-scale smuggling across state lines—and it's a multibillion-dollar business. A single truckload of cigarettes bought in a low-tax state like Virginia and illegally sold in a high-tax state like New York can yield several million dollars in profit.

Cigarette smuggling across international borders is also a serious problem. Often, these operations involve the smuggling of counterfeit cigarettes—fakes in fake name-brand boxes, often containing substances even more harmful than tobacco.

A typical case of international smuggling is one from the summer of 2011. Working out of a field division office in Seattle, Washington, the bureau partnered with other federal and local agencies to bust a major operation involving cigarettes smuggled from Vietnam. Before it was stopped, the illegal operation cost the United States an estimated $24 million in lost tax revenues. In a statement after the bust (quoted in an article in the Seattle Police Department's newsletter), ATF Special Agent in Charge Kelvin Crenshaw commented,

Trafficking in contraband cigarettes deceives and defrauds consumers and steals income from legitimate businesses. The execution of today's search warrants represents a commitment by both ATF and its partners to identify, investigate and pursue individuals that would look to commit schemes that defraud our governments and ultimately rob our communities. We will continue to aggressively pursue those who violate federal law and defraud the state of Washington.

FIREARMS ENFORCEMENT

Although the ATF is indeed charged with regulating the manufacture, sale, and distribution of firearms, its main focus is on investigating crimes.

The ATF tackles the problem from several angles. In part, it maintains a number of facilities devoted to specific aspects of gun crime investigation. One of these is the National Tracing Center (NTC), which is headquartered in Martinsburg, West Virginia. This center tracks firearms from manufacturer to purchaser, both internationally and within the United States.

The NTC and other groups within the ATF and elsewhere make use of an enormous database called the National Integrated Ballistic Identification Network (NIBIN). NIBIN stores millions of pieces of information about firearms that may have been illegally used. It is kept up to date as law enforcement agencies provide new information on such details of **ballistics** as fired ammunition and the marks inside the barrels of crime guns. (A "crime gun" is defined as any firearm that is illegally possessed,

The ATF's National Integrated Ballistic Information Network (NIBIN) has proved to be an effective tool in apprehending suspects in gun-related crimes. NIBIN is a huge database that compiles and stores ballistics information connected to crime scenes. This information can then be cross-checked to find matches indicating that the same weapon has been used in more than one crime.

As of 2012, more than 1.6 million pieces of crime scene evidence were in the system and more than 34,700 matches had been made. Many of these matches yielded investigative information that would otherwise not have come to light. Here are a few cases that succeeded in part because of NIBIN.

In October 2004, the Philadelphia (Pennsylvania) Police Department responded to a drug-related shooting during which one victim was shot three times. From 2004 to 2006, the ATF led a complex undercover task force investigation of the "Take Down Records Gang," an armed drug trafficking group that operated in Philadelphia, Baltimore, New Jersey, and Delaware. Using NIBIN, the Philadelphia Police Department linked two pistols obtained during two searches to the shooting incident. Federal prosecutors were then able to connect the shooting to a much larger operation. In the end, according to NIBIN, the task force on this case delivered thirty-three search warrants, recovered thirty-three firearms, and seized more than $1.2 million in cash. Ultimately, fourteen defendants pleaded guilty to federal firearms violations, drug trafficking, conspiracy, or money laundering. The leader of the conspiracy was sentenced to life imprisonment.

In May 2003, the Washington County (Minnesota) Sheriff's Department and Oakdale (Minnesota) Police Department investigated the shooting of a driver during an attempted carjacking. Soon after, officers identified a second carjacking incident. The next day, the Hudson (Wisconsin) Police Department responded to an armored car robbery during which the criminal, driving the carjacked vehicle, took an estimated $238,000 in cash.

Five years later, in 2008, a routine traffic stop led to a driver's arrest for unlawful possession of a firearm with an obliterated serial number. A criminal history check identified the suspect as a felon. Using NIBIN, the Minneapolis police then linked the firearm to the earlier carjacking shooting. In addition, the ATF traced the firearm to a single buyer. The Polk County (Wisconsin) Sheriff's Office then served a search warrant at the buyer's home, recovered evidence of the armored car robbery, and arrested a suspect. A year later, in 2009, that suspect

was sentenced to twelve years for attempted murder and carjacking. Prosecution for the armored car robbery was still pending as of 2011.

On April 16, 2008, the Wilmington (Delaware) Police Department responded to an incident involving a victim who was shot and killed on a sidewalk. That same day, the New Castle County (Delaware) Police Department stopped a vehicle for a traffic violation, recovered a .32 caliber revolver, and arrested both occupants of the car for unlawful possession of a firearm. Using NIBIN, the Delaware State Police Forensic Firearms Service Unit could link the firearm to the homicide. Both suspects were charged with murder, robbery, and state firearms violations. In 2009, following guilty pleas to manslaughter, the defendants each received a sentence of fifteen years' imprisonment.

From 2003 to 2006, the Albany (New York) Police Department responded to forty shootings, including eight gang-related attempted murders. At each scene, officers collected spent ammunition from six firearms. As a result, the Albany police arrested two members of an organization called the Jungle Junkies Gang for unlawful possession of firearms.

Using NIBIN, officers were able to link one pistol to four of the shootings and the other to four other shootings. The ATF formed a joint task force with the FBI, DEA, the Albany Police Department, and the U.S. Attorney General's Office to investigate the Jungle Junkies Gang. Two search warrants and thirty arrests resulted from this investigation. Meanwhile, federal authorities prosecuted all eight attempted murders as RICO crimes. (RICO stands for Racketeer Influenced and Corrupt Organizations Act, a law designed to prosecute organized crime syndicates.) From 2006 to 2009, twenty-nine of the thirty defendants pleaded guilty. The thirtieth defendant was convicted by a trial jury. Sentences for the defendants were as high as fifteen years' imprisonment.

Above: Ohio-based ATF agent Wayne Dixie Jr. displays some of the many guns that were retrieved from a 2005 gun-trafficking case.

used in a crime, or suspected of having been used in a crime.) Ballistics information can then be used to match ammunition to firearms, and to identify firearms that may have been used in separate crimes.

Also headquartered in Martinsburg are many highly focused teams devoted to the monitoring of firearms. For example, one group keeps tabs on gun shops that have gone out of business, in order to ensure that the owners had complied with regulations about the final sale and distribution of their merchandise.

Another group is the bureau's Firearms Technology Branch (FTB), its technical authority on firearms. Among the FTB's duties are testing and evaluating firearms, providing expert testimony, supervising the control of firearms made overseas, and maintaining extensive reference files. As with NIBIN, the FTB's services are available to a wide range of groups and people outside the bureau, including federal and local law enforcement agencies, the firearms industry, Congress, and the general public.

EXPLOSIVES AND BOMBING CASES

Then there's the related issue of explosives. Much of the ATF's work in this field involves overseeing the legal manufacture and use of explosive or **incendiary** materials. The vast majority of explosive material is used in the mining industry, but many other businesses also rely on it. For example, explosives are key to such industries as oil exploration, avalanche control, the production of fire extinguishers and car airbags, fireworks, and special effects for movies and concerts. Proper control is crucial, and ATF investigators issue licenses to, and oversee, roughly 11,000 businesses every year.

Of course, not everyone uses explosives or incendiary devices legally, so the ATF maintains a number of facilities and programs devoted to investigating bombing incidents and preventing future ones. One example is the U.S. Bomb Data Center. Like NIBIN for firearms, the Bomb Data Center compiles statistics and other information from federal and local agencies around the country. It then makes the data available to law enforcement agencies through a secure website.

Using this information, agencies can study details of the manufacture and detonation of specific bombs without viewing the physical evidence. This allows the agencies to search for patterns and similarities among cases, which in turn can lead to important investigative leads. The same is true in cases of arson.

Since the ATF has such large-scale resources at its disposal, and is larger and better funded than local law enforcement agencies, it can make a significant difference in solving a bombing or arson case. A terrorist attack in Atlanta during the 1996 Summer Olympics is a prominent example of this capability. The explosion occurred in Atlanta's Centennial Park, where thousands had gathered for an outdoor concert. The device responsible was the largest pipe bomb yet recorded—40 pounds (about 18 kilograms) of explosive material surrounded by nails and placed in an army field pack. When the bomb was detonated, the blast killed two people and injured more than one hundred.

The FBI and the ATF, together with several other agencies, were immediately called in. They secured the area and soon

When a bomb went off during the 1996 Summer Olympics in Atlanta, Georgia, the ATF was called in to investigate.

went to work analyzing the bomb fragments and interviewing thousands of witnesses. The agencies later linked the deadly bombing with three other explosions that had occurred shortly after the Centennial Park incident at two abortion clinics and a lesbian bar.

The perpetrator was identified as a man named Eric Rudolph, and a reward of $1 million was posted. However, he avoided capture for five years by hiding in the mountainous Appalachian region, an area Rudolph knew well. After his capture, he stated that his reasons for the attacks were to protest the excesses of government (which the Olympics represented to him), and to stop abortion and take away the rights of homosexuals. Rudolph also told investigators where to find massive stores of explosives he had hidden. Agents found this material and neutralized it. In exchange for revealing his information, Rudolph was given a life sentence rather than the death penalty.

GETTING HOOKED ON FORENSIC CHEMISTRY

ATF forensic chemist Michelle Ricketts Reardon has a particular focus: C4 explosives. She devised a way to isolate the chemical compounds that differentiate one batch of this highly dangerous explosive from another. Reardon's technique gives scientists the ability to match traces of C4 found at a crime scene with other batches.

The discovery was an important breakthrough. Because of it, in 2006, at the age of thirty, Reardon was given a prestigious honor called the Arthur S. Flemming Award, which recognizes outstanding work in the federal government. She was the first ATF employee to be given this honor.

At an early age, Reardon became interested in a career that could combine chemistry and law enforcement. She recalls,

> I was an avid reader. In middle school I started reading a lot of Patricia Cornwell mystery novels. Her early books sparked my interest in forensics. She wrote about this fictional medical examiner named Kay Scarpetta who was good at solving murders. So for awhile I really wanted to be a medical examiner. And this was back in the 80's, before the whole CSI craze.
>
> [However,] I knew I would have to take anatomy classes. I realized that if I couldn't cut into a bloodworm in high school biology class, then I definitely wouldn't be able to handle a human. So I started looking into other areas of forensics that would require minimal contact with victims.
>
> In high school I began to get serious about the chemistry side of forensics. I had a wonderful chemistry teacher who was a big influence on me. Her enthusiasm and love of chemistry were inspiring. We developed a great rapport. She helped me focus on what I wanted to do in life.

EMERGENCY TEAMS

The Rudolph case was an example of the ATF's role in directly intervening in major crimes. At the forefront of these investigations is the bureau's National Response Team (NRT), the team that responded to the East Texas church arsons. Retired fire investigator Ed Comeau, writing in the magazine of the National Fire Protection Association, comments,

> Any fire investigation, no matter how small, requires a range of skills and disciplines. A smaller incident may be investigated by a few people from the local fire department or state fire marshal's office. If an incident is of such catastrophic proportions that an investigation would exceed the abilities of the local authority, however, there's a resource to call upon: the Bureau of Alcohol, Tobacco and Firearms' (ATF) National Response Team (NRT).

Besides the Atlanta Olympics, East Texas, and Oklahoma City bombings, the NRT has helped with many other disasters, including the terrorist attacks of 9/11; an abortion clinic bombing in Birmingham, Alabama, in 1998; and an explosion at the Imperial Sugar Refinery in Port Wentworth, Georgia, in 2008. Another example of a crisis in which the NRT lent its resources and manpower was a fire at an apartment complex in Bremerton, Washington, that resulted in four deaths. That city's fire chief, Al Duke, commented, "The ATF brings resources to bear on an incident that [are] simply not available within our department. We would have been there three weeks trying to dig out the scene."

Associated with the NRT is the International Response Team (IRT). As the name implies, this team is the equivalent of the NRT on an international scale. It stands ready to help the Bureau of Diplomatic Security (DS), the State Department's security and law enforcement arm, as well as the governments of other countries, in the wake of major arson or bombings.

For example, in 2003 the IRT helped in the aftermath of a nightclub bombing in Bogotá, Colombia, that killed thirty-two people. The team also responded to an explosion in an Albanian ammunition depot that resulted in twenty-six deaths, the wounding of about four hundred people, and the destruction or damage of more than four thousand homes and businesses. The IRT has taken part in many other overseas operations as well, including investigating large-vehicle bombings and disassembling improvised explosive devices (IEDs).

In addition to the NRT and IRT, the bureau maintains many more specialized teams. For example, there are the K-9 (dog) teams in its Explosives Detection Canine program. The Labrador retrievers used in this program are specially trained to detect explosives and **accelerants**. ATF also supplies training programs to other law enforcement agencies that maintain their own K-9 teams.

Sandman, a yellow Labrador retriever, is being trained to detect explosives.

LONG-RANGE PROGRAMS

Unlike the NRT or K-9 programs, some of ATF's subgroups don't deal directly with crisis intervention. Instead, they focus on longer-range goals of research and community aid.

For example, some of the bureau's special agents work at the National Center for the Analysis of Violent Crime (NCAVC), which is operated by the Federal Bureau of Investigation at its headquarters in Quantico, Virginia. This center's mission is to study information about repetitive violent crimes, looking at patterns and creating profiles of possible offenders. ATF agents get involved when these crimes are part of the bureau's responsibilities.

Other ATF programs have similar partnerships with other law enforcement agencies. One example is a task force called the Violent Crime Impact Team (VCIT). It focuses on reducing gun violence in neighborhoods that are experiencing especially heavy crime because of the activities of street gangs or home invasion crews.

As of 2012, there are about thirty VCIT teams around the country. Each team includes special agents, intelligence research specialists, and investigative assistants from the ATF, as well as representatives from local organizations, such as law enforcement agencies, social service organizations, and schools. The local organizations and law enforcement agencies supply knowledge of local offenders and crime "hot spots." Meanwhile, the ATF supplies resources and personnel for such operations as undercover work, contact with confidential informants, and the identification and apprehension of offenders.

The results are striking. Since it began in 2004, the VCIT program has been responsible for the arrests of more than 13,400 gang members, drug dealers, felons in possession of firearms, and other violent criminals. It has also recovered more than 16,440 firearms. Furthermore, statistics indicate that neighborhoods with active VCIT programs consistently outperform the national average in terms of arrests and convictions.

SUPPORT JOBS

To carry out programs like the VCIT project, as well as to effectively perform the rest of their responsibilities, special agents and investigators rely on a large network of other ATF employees. Thousands of people apply yearly to be special agents or investigators, but only a handful can be hired. Luckily, there are many other job opportunities within the ATF. All of them provide services that are vital to keeping the bureau working smoothly and efficiently.

Some of these employees have relatively specialized positions. They are professionals such as ballistics experts, information technology experts, and forensic chemists. Other ATF employees, meanwhile, have duties that can be similar to those you'd see in any large organization or company. This category of support staff is a broad one, and includes such positions as the following:

- Administration personnel (human resources, office management, finance, law, data processing, as well as records management, etc.)

- Equipment managers
- Lab assistants
- Linguists (who transcribe, translate, and analyze materials not written or spoken in English)
- Other support personnel (for graphic arts, automotive maintenance, public affairs, etc.)
- Surveillance technicians

All these jobs are necessary because the scope of the ATF's role is so broad. If you're interested in taking part in this challenging work, it's never too early to start learning about it.

WHAT'S NEEDED TO JOIN THE ATF?

ONCE YOU'VE LEARNED ABOUT THE WORK THE ATF does, it'll be time to find out more about joining it. The best place to start is the official website: www.atf.gov, which has extensive details about the bureau and career opportunities there. If you're interested in getting some active, hands-on experience in what the ATF does, check out Law Enforcement Career Exploring. The Exploring program is part of a national organization that matches students between fourteen and twenty years old with a range of law enforcement agencies, including regional field offices of the ATF.

By joining an Exploring program, you'll experience situations that full-fledged ATF employees encounter, learn about the equipment they use, and gain confidence and knowledge in such areas as leadership, marksmanship, and emergency aid for accidents and disasters. Your schedule as an Explorer will fit around your school schedule. You can find out more about Exploring programs at the site of the nonprofit agency (part

ATF special agents training people on how to shoot weapons properly.

of the Boy Scouts of America) that oversees them: http://exploring. learningforlife.org/services/career-exploring/law-enforcement/.

INTERNSHIPS

As you move into high school and college, you can get an even better taste of what life will be like as an ATF employee. You can take part in the ATF's internship opportunities for students, which are grouped together as the Student Educational Employment Program (SEEP). As an intern, you'll work alongside real ATF employees. Much of the work you'll do will be clerical, but even so you'll have a chance to be part of a working ATF office. An added bonus: you can usually get school credit for participating.

An internship can be a powerful force in deciding your future career. Six out of ten students who have gone through the ATF's internship programs have returned to the bureau at some point in their careers. Keep in mind that going through a SEEP program doesn't guarantee that you'll get a job. However, you will be in a good position if you should decide to apply. You'll get important experience, and ATF recruiters will know what you can offer. Senior Operations Officer Brenda Jefferson, who ran ATF's student volunteer program, commented, "Although the internships do not convert [automatically switch over] to career positions, they're still invaluable."

There are three basic components to SEEP: the Student Career Experience Program (SCEP), the Student Temporary Employment Program (STEP), and the Student Volunteer Program (SVP).

SCEP is for students who are already working toward a career in law enforcement by majoring in a field such as criminology. SCEP typically encompasses 640 hours of work and study over two school years and the summer in between. (You may be able to waive half of these hours if your grade point average is 3.5 or higher.) SCEP has certain basic requirements. You must

- Be a U.S. citizen, or national, or a noncitizen who is legally eligible for employment
- Be able to pass a background check (because you'll need security clearance)
- Be at least sixteen years old when your appointment begins
- Be enrolled full-time at an **accredited** high school leading to a diploma (or have earned a GED), or at a two- or four-year vocational institute or college, in a field of study related to the position for which you are applying

- Be registered with the military Selective Service or exempt if you are a male between the ages of eighteen and twenty-five
- Get a written agreement from your school
- Maintain a 3.0 or better grade point average
- Not be the son or daughter of a current ATF employee

STEP AND SVP INTERNSHIPS

In some ways, the STEP program is more flexible than SCEP. This is because the work you'll do doesn't have to relate directly to your academic goals. In other words, you can study any subject and still be an intern. Also, the grade requirements are not as strict. As with SCEP, the work will be spread out, usually over two school years and the summer in between.

STEP's requirements are slightly different from SCEP's. You must

- Be a U.S. citizen, or national, or a noncitizen who is legally eligible for employment
- Be able to pass a background check (because you'll need security clearance)
- Be able to type at least forty words per minute
- Be at least sixteen years old when your appointment begins
- Be enrolled at least half-time as a degree-seeking student in an educational program accredited by a recognized body

- Be registered with the military Selective Service or exempt if you are a male between the ages of eighteen and twenty-five
- Get a written agreement from your school
- Maintain a 2.0 or better grade point average
- Not be a son or daughter of a current ATF employee

ATF's third internship opportunity is called the Student Volunteer Program (SVP). As the name suggests, this internship is unpaid. (Both STEP and SCEP offer salaries and some benefits.) As with the ATF's other internships, the SVP plan is designed to fit around your regular school schedule. You'll typically work a minimum of twelve hours per week for one or two semesters, two quarters, or a summer session.

To be considered for SVP, you must

- Be a U.S. citizen, or national, or a noncitizen who is legally eligible for employment
- Be able to pass a background check (because you'll need security clearance)
- Be at least sixteen years old when your appointment begins
- Be enrolled at least half-time as a degree-seeking student in an educational program accredited by a recognized body
- Be registered with the military Selective Service or exempt if you are a male between the ages of eighteen and twenty-five

AN INTERN CHASES STOLEN GUNS

In 2010, Carter Cole did something interesting during one semester of her senior year at Sam Houston State University in Huntsville, Texas. She tracked stolen guns as an intern in ATF's field office in Houston, Texas. Some of her time was spent in the office chasing paper trails, but she also took part in surveillance missions. Interns like Cole have a chance to do a variety of other things as well, such as visiting gun vaults where technicians test-fire weapons, assist in educational sessions for law enforcement agencies, and take part in conferences related to ATF's work.

Cole says that the experience hooked her on a future in investigative work. This excerpt from an article published on her university's website provides more details:

[Cole says,] "It has been very interesting. There are a lot of agents working their way up from the small people to the big guys."

Texas is the number one source state of crime guns recovered in Mexico and Houston is the number one city within Texas, said Special Agent Dr. Franceska Perot, the public information officer for the Houston Field Office. "The drugs are coming up from Mexico, and the guns and money are moving back down. We work the weapons like DEA (Drug Enforcement Agency) works drugs—we are after the transportation and supply."

[Cole says,] "When I first started working here, I watched how things were done. It looked like they are really making an impact. I got to meet all different kinds of people. Some were police officers before they came to ATF, and some were right out of college. I met agents from New York and California as well as several agents for the DEA and ICE (Immigration and Customs Enforcement)."

The paperwork in cases, although not the exciting part of the job, is critical for the conviction of gunrunners. It helps to track stolen weapons or straw purchases, where buyers use an intermediary to purchase a firearm from a licensed dealer to hide their identity. With 1,500 licensed gun dealers in the Houston region, and 5,000 in the Southern region, it is a huge and tedious task.

"I would hire her in a minute," said Special Agent Daniel Casey, a Group Supervisor in Houston who supervised Cole. "She gets along with everyone and doesn't hold [back] her opinions, but she does it in a professional way. I think she would make a good employee.

"At the ATF, it requires a lot of hard work and a desire to succeed," Casey said. "There has to be a drive within you to go out at 1 or 3 am . . . on surveillance. There are a lot of times that the job supersedes family events. You have to make personal sacrifices."

- Get a written agreement from your school
- Maintain a 2.0 or better grade point average
- Not be a son or daughter of a current ATF
  employee

BASIC REQUIREMENTS FOR SUPPORT JOBS

Of course, you don't have to be an intern to apply for a position with the ATF. However, as with the internship programs, you will need to meet certain basic conditions. Regardless of any given requirements for a specific position, all ATF applicants have to meet certain basic criteria. You must

- Be a U.S. citizen
- Be able to handle the physical demands of the position you're applying for
- Be registered with the military Selective Service or exempt if you are a male between the ages of eighteen and twenty-five
- Have a high school diploma or GED (General Educational Development) equivalent
- Have a valid driver's license (there are some exceptions to this)
- Pass a thorough background investigation to obtain a security clearance
- Pass general medical and mental health tests and a drug test, as well as meet the bureau's overall drug policy

Beyond these basics, specific jobs will have specific prerequisites. For example, fingerprint classifiers are essentially assistants to senior fingerprint analysts. They handle the more routine aspects of day-to-day operations, such as fingerprinting suspects and others, preparing reports, and cataloging and storing samples.

In addition to the minimum requirements for all ATF employees, in order to fill this position you would need at least a year of directly related professional experience, a master's or equivalent graduate degree, two full years of graduate-level education in a related field, or a satisfactory combination of education and experience.

PREREQUISITES FOR SPECIAL AGENTS AND INVESTIGATORS

Positions as investigators and special agents have much stricter requirements. Competition is strong among the many applicants for these positions. Only a tiny percentage of candidates who meet the basic requirements are hired.

The most basic prerequisites for being an investigator are not very different from the general basic requirements for support positions. You must

- Be a U.S. citizen
- Be able to handle the physical requirements of the position
- Be prepared to travel up to about half of every month if necessary
- Be registered with the military Selective Service

or exempt if you are a male between the ages of
eighteen and twenty-five
- Have a valid driver's license
- Pass a thorough background investigation to obtain
a security clearance
- Pass general medical and mental health tests and
a drug test, as well as meet the bureau's overall
drug policy

If you're hoping to be a special agent, you'll need to meet
still more criteria. At a minimum, you'll also have to

- Be at least twenty-one and not older than thirty-six
when you start your job
- Have a bachelor's degree or higher from an accredited college or university (or an equivalent combination of education and experience)
- Pass special exams and assessment tests (physical,
mental, general knowledge), and have three or more
years of experience in criminal investigation or law
enforcement agencies; or possess a combination of
education and related experience in a law enforcement field

EXPERIENCE AND EDUCATION

ATF recruiters, who have a certain amount of flexibility regarding the education-and-experience requirement, will decide on a
case-by-case basis if you have the right combination. Generally,
it's not enough to have been a uniformed officer. You'll need

at least a few years' experience of police work in which your main duties included actively using investigative techniques and working on major crimes.

In terms of the educational component, it's not necessary to have a degree in criminal justice. In fact, some recruiters feel that it is better to have a well-rounded education, with a major in something else. (This is true for other law enforcement agencies as well.) In their opinion, since being an ATF special agent requires a wide range of skills, a solid grounding in different subjects is best.

For example, you might want to study some combination of math, computer science or other science, foreign languages, communication, psychology, sociology, and/or law and government. You certainly don't need to study all of these—it would be a very unusual person who did. But some combination will be a plus. Furthermore, although not required, it will be beneficial if you have other skills to bring to the job. For example, you might be bilingual or skilled in a martial art.

APPLYING

If you meet the basic requirements for a job, you can start the application process. Once again, the first place to visit will be the ATF's extensive website, specifically the section devoted to careers: www.atf.gov/careers/opportunities/.

You can also go to the federal government's central site for job applications, www.usajobs.gov. This site posts available job categories and details such as responsibilities, salary, location, and requirements. It's important to check these listings regularly. Generally, job announcements remain open for several weeks, although some go quickly and some hard-to-fill positions may stay open longer.

You can also sign up to receive e-mail announcements of new openings, and the public information officer at the ATF regional field office nearest you can help. He or she can answer your questions (or direct you to someone who can). For a link to a list of field offices and contact information, visit www.atf.gov/contact/.

Your next step will be to create an online application. This is the basic application used for all federal jobs. You'll be able to customize it, so that it will be appropriate for the particular job you're applying for. The first portion of the application will ask you to provide basic information. Essentially, it will verify that you do meet the minimum requirements. At the same time, no matter what job within the ATF you're seeking, you'll need to create or update your **résumé** and submit it. You may be asked to provide other materials as well, such as a personal essay.

At this point, assuming you meet all the minimum requirements, the process will continue. During this period, it will be important to have regular access to a computer so that the ATF can keep in touch with you. Bear in mind that the bureau receives thousands of applications every year and is unable to tell you the status of your individual application. However, you can assume that you're still in the system unless told in writing that you're no longer being considered.

If ATF recruiters decide that your application looks promising, you'll be asked to start the testing and interview process. This is typically carried out at a regional field office, although other arrangements can be made if necessary.

For your interview, make sure you come prepared. (Of course, this advice is good for any job interview.) Practice answering questions with friends if you think it will be helpful. Pay attention to your appearance, and be polite and attentive. This may seem obvious, but recruiters say that they're always surprised at how many people ignore these ground rules for making a positive impression.

If you're applying to become a special agent, there will be considerably more testing than the basics. In addition to face-to-face interviews, the process will include a drug screening test and a polygraph (lie detector) test. Furthermore, you'll be subject to an increasingly tough series of written and oral exams. These will include a particular test called the Special Agent Exam. It will test your skills in verbal reasoning, quantitative reasoning, and investigative reasoning. For sample questions that will help you with this test, visit the ATF website's section on the exam: www.atf.gov/careers/special-agents/exam-203-samples.html.

PHYSICAL AND MENTAL TESTING

It's no surprise that special agent candidates will also need to be in excellent mental and physical health. For obvious reasons, as a special agent you'll need to be in top shape—and stay there.

Consider just the mental health requirements. As a special agent, you'll need to have a number of positive mental and emotional qualities. For example, the ability to stay levelheaded and think clearly in intense or dangerous situations will be crucial. You'll need to be able to work well, both alone and in teams. And you'll need to be respectful of the many different

WRITING A RÉSUMÉ

If you apply for an internship or a position with the ATF, you will need to write a résumé. (The same is true, of course, when you're applying for any job.) A good resumé will provide details about your qualifications and experience, and explain why you think you are the right person.

You will also need to write a cover letter. Keep this concise, maybe three or four paragraphs. The idea is to convey as much information as possible in a small space. It's an opportunity to introduce yourself and demonstrate your enthusiasm. Don't be afraid to brag a little—this is one time when that's acceptable. On the other hand, avoid sounding arrogant or self-absorbed.

A cover letter should be customized as much as possible. For instance, if you can, learn the name of the person who will be reading your submission. It's much better to start with "Dear Mr. or Ms. . . . " than with an impersonal phrase like "To whom it may concern." Close your cover letter by thanking the recipient for considering you.

Along with the cover letter, send your résumé. Typically, this will include the following:

- Contact information
- Education and training details
- Work experience and other experience
- Any other qualifications (such as awards or special abilities)
- References

Finally, remember that neatness counts. Your cover letter and résumé should be clearly written, with no misspellings, bad grammar, typographical mistakes, or other errors. Recruiters say that you'd be surprised at how many sloppy applications come their way.

If you're going to hit a target, you need to have excellent eyesight.

kinds of people you'll encounter on the job. As for the physical requirements, the bureau's website notes,

> The job of an ATF Special Agent can be dangerous and physically demanding, and being physically fit can sometimes mean the difference between life and death. Applicants for the position of special agent must be able to demonstrate that they are in excellent physical condition and are able to perform tasks such as defensive tactics, arrest techniques and proficient use of firearms.

One example of the general health requirements is your eyesight. You'll need uncorrected distance vision of at least 20/100 in each eye; corrected (with glasses) distance vision of

WHAT'S NEEDED TO JOIN THE ATF?

at least 20/20 in one eye and 20/30 in the other. Normal depth perception and peripheral vision are also required, and color blindness isn't acceptable.

In addition to this and other general health requirements, you'll need to pass a standardized fitness exam called a Physical Task Test (PTT). Failure to meet the minimum standards in any of the tested areas will disqualify you from the application process—and there are no second chances.

The test will consist of three parts, with minimal resting in between. As of 2012, the standards for applicants twenty-one to twenty-nine years old were

- A 1.5-mile (2.41-kilometer) run (with a minimum time of 12:19 for men and 15:36 for women)
- Push-ups (a minimum of thirty-three for men and sixteen for women within one minute)
- Sit-ups (a minimum of forty for men and thirty-five for women within one minute)

CHECKING YOUR BACKGROUND

In addition to the physical testing, a major segment of the screening process will consist of a background check. This will give ATF recruiters a chance to know more about you by looking at aspects of your past and present life. The purpose is to create a full picture of your personality, strengths, and weaknesses. Recruiters will consider questions like these: What's your overall character? What life experiences do you have? Have you been involved in community or school activities that indicate a commitment to society? Do you have a strong work ethic? Will you be comfortable working odd hours if needed or in unpredictable environments?

In order to answer these questions, the recruiters will interview your family, coworkers, and friends. They'll also check your financial records to look for problems. For example, large outstanding loans will be of concern, since they could indicate a vulnerability to bribery or corruption.

ATF recruiters will also look at your police record. If any serious problems come to light, such as a felony conviction, you'll be immediately disqualified. As for drug use: not surprisingly, current or recent drug usage will disqualify you. So will a previous conviction, if it was for manufacturing, distributing, or selling an illegal drug.

However, there is some leeway about drug use. Generally speaking, the bureau wants to see, at most, what it calls "minimal experimental usage" during your lifetime. ATF recruiters consider minor drug use on a case-by-case basis, so casual drug use in the past will not automatically disqualify you, but it won't be a plus.

Altogether, the background check is very thorough. It will even include a look at what you have posted on social networking sites and discussion forums. Anything that might put you in a negative light is a potential problem. (This is increasingly true for many employers in or out of law enforcement.) The rule of thumb is don't post anything that you wouldn't say in person to someone like your parents, a police officer, or a job recruiter.

Here's another valuable rule of thumb: don't lie. If you do, you're sure to be found out—remember, the background check is thorough. The ATF can't take a chance on hiring someone who may be a risk or who has a questionable past. And it certainly won't hire someone who would falsify information.

Although exceptional physical fitness is a requirement to be a special agent, this is not necessarily so for investigators, professionals, or support staff. For example, there is no reason a person who uses a wheelchair cannot be a forensic scientist, secretary, or accountant. As with all federal agencies, the bureau does not discriminate on the basis of physical disability. The same is true for discrimination on the basis of sex, sexual orientation, parental status, religion, or race.

Clearly, not everyone who applies to the bureau is hired, if only because there are always more applicants than there are job openings in any capacity. But if you're determined and make it through the battery of tests, background checks, and interviews, you'll stand a good chance of starting work. You're still not there, however. Even if you're hired, you'll need some training first.

THREE

ON THE JOB

THE SPECIFIC TRAINING A NEW EMPLOYEE RECEIVES depends on the job. However, some of it will be general instruction for all new employees. This will cover a wide range of topics, such as the ATF's workplace policies, the bureau's overall mission, and its standards of conduct. More specifically, you'll learn about topics such as making the best use of your resources, instruments, tools, and equipment.

The length of your training period will vary. Some support staff may need only a few weeks or even less. On the other hand, for future special agents and investigators, the training period will incorporate months of demanding work and intense study, calling for a steep learning curve.

SPECIAL AGENT TRAINING

If you become a special agent, your training period will last for twenty-seven weeks. This is longer than that of any other Department of Justice special agent: that is, even longer than

An ATF agent stands in a bombed apartment during a post-bomb-training exercise as part of a practice course in sharpening agents' bomb investigation skills.

the programs run by the Federal Bureau of Investigation, Drug Enforcement Agency, or the U.S. Marshals Service. It will take place at the Federal Law Enforcement Training Center (FLETC) in Glynco, Georgia. The training includes a week of "pre-basic" orientation, twelve weeks of general criminal investigation training, and fifteen weeks of courses specifically for future special agents.

FLETC Glynco is a busy place. About ninety federal agencies besides ATF use its facilities, as well as other law enforcement agencies from the United States and abroad. It's also huge—big enough to have its own zip code and to house about 3,500 students at a time. The 1,600-acre FLETC campus has outdoor training grounds for such activities as firearms practice, driver training, explosives training, arson investigation, and rescue via helicopter and other methods. Physical workout facilities alone cover three acres.

There's even a full-size mock neighborhood, complete with dozens of fake structures and a port of entry (essentially, a false airport terminal), restaurants and bars, pawnshops, a courtroom for practicing expert testimony—even a fake moonshine still. You'll use this "neighborhood" to study surveillance, apprehension, and other techniques, with local actors playing both offenders and civilians during the exercises.

Indoors, there are classrooms in which you'll study such topics as interviewing and apprehension techniques, law (notably, the body of legal practice built up around the Fourth Amendment to the Constitution regarding illegal search and seizure), surveillance, and first aid. Communication skills are also stressed. This is because special agents and many other ATF employees are frequently asked to report on their work, either in writing or by briefing your colleagues orally. And sometimes you'll appear in court to give expert testimony— that is, to explain your experiences and conclusions. So an important part of your day-to-day work will be to communicate clearly, accurately, and concisely.

FLETC Glynco has a library, dormitories, a dining hall, and laboratories for hands-on instruction in computer forensics, fingerprinting, identifying narcotics, and other topics.

Naturally, maintaining physical fitness will also be part of your training. In fact, you'll be tested the first week with the same physical fitness test you passed during the application process. You'll be tested again at periodic intervals during your training, and if you fail at any point you'll be ousted from the program.

MORE TRAINING

In addition to your twenty-seven weeks at Glynco, you might need even more training if you are planning to have a particular specialty. For example, to be a Certified Fire Investigator (CFI), you'll go through additional training at the U.S. Fire Administration's National Fire Academy in Emmitsburg, Maryland.

There, you'll learn techniques such as determining the origin and cause of a fire, as well as fire dynamics, computer modeling of fires, how various building materials affect fire, and fire-event-related health and safety. Mark D. Jones, the now-retired branch chief of the bureau's Arson & Explosives Intelligence Branch, comments, "The goal for these agents is to be able to walk into a building that has experienced a fire and make an unequivocal determination as to its cause and origin."

Similarly, if you join the bureau's K-9 explosives detection squad, you'll have five weeks of training at the ATF's Canine Training Center in Front Royal, Virginia. Your four-footed future partner, meanwhile, will have ten weeks of training, learning to detect the odors of chemical compounds used in some 19,000 formulas. When this exceptional animal's training is complete it will be, in the words of the ATF, "an extremely versatile, mobile, and accurate explosives detection tool."

Other examples of training are the courses required to become an expert in bombings, as either an explosives enforcement officer (EEO) or certified explosives specialist (CES). Often, people in these positions have already had years of experience as explosives disposal technicians in the military. Some of the extra training they'll get with the ATF will take place at the Hazardous Devices

School of the Redstone Arsenal, which is maintained by the FBI and the U.S. Army in Huntsville, Alabama. The FBI's website states that students in Huntsville learn explosives "[f]rom A to Z," through such courses as the following:

> The fundamentals of explosives. How to recognize hazardous devices, assess them, and either render them safe or explode them without endangering life or property. Post-blast investigations (what exploded and why). Decontamination and disposal procedures. Basic electronics. Fragment analysis. The latest on protective clothing. Specialty courses on state-of-the-art robots. . . . For executives, the ins and outs of managing a bomb squad. And cutting edge counterterrorism bomb training on how to respond to suicide attacks, large vehicle bombs, weapons of mass destruction, and mortar attacks.

Meanwhile, the basic training period for investigators is somewhat less rigorous than for special agents. It typically lasts about nine weeks, although more time may be needed in some cases. Among the things you'll study are techniques for apprehension and surveillance, identifying makes of firearms and explosives, helping legitimate businesses obtain and update their licenses, confirming that businesses are complying with regulations, using high-tech instruments to detect hidden firearms or explosives, and courtroom testimony in cases that may result in a company's license being **revoked**.

No matter what job you're aiming for, when your course

of training is over, you'll have a proud moment at your graduation ceremony. Then you'll be ready to start work. When you begin work, you'll have to undergo a probationary period, which is typically two or three years for special agents and investigators. During this period, a senior employee will oversee the work you do, making sure that it meets the right standards. Your supervisor will also guide you as you become more comfortable with the position, and see that you're fitting in well with the overall organization.

Then the real work starts.

As any law enforcement officer will tell you, being out in the real world—that is, on the job—is very different from being in school or a training program, or even in a probationary period when more experienced people are guiding you. Doing the work on your own will be a whole new experience.

One thing is certain if you choose a career with the ATF: it won't be dull. Especially if you're a special agent or an investigator, you won't be doing the same thing day after day. One day you may take part in a surveillance operation. On another, you might interview witnesses in a bombing case. You may need to obtain and execute a search warrant for a suspected stash of weapons. Or perhaps you'll search for physical evidence or make an arrest in the wake of an arson incident.

BOMBING SPECIALISTS

In large part, the specific daily responsibilities of a bombing specialist will depend on your particular area of expertise—in other words, the subspecialty you choose within the overall categories of special agents and investigators.

For instance, you might choose to work for ATF's Explosives Technology Branch. Some members of this department focus on prevention. Their duties include advising agencies on storage regulations and proper handling procedures for explosives and incendiaries; investigating the theft of explosive materials; and gauging threat levels. This last facet of the job includes procedures such as checking for weaknesses in buildings, and finding ways to strengthen the structures. This is especially important in situations where the threat level may be high, as is often the case during major political events.

Meanwhile, other members of the Explosives Technology Branch focus primarily on the aftermath of disasters. They respond to explosions, conduct recovery and disposal operations, and investigate the cause of a bombing or explosion.

Explosives experts from the ATF often travel far afield to do their work—sometimes across oceans. For instance, in 2010 a

Investigators examine the massive amounts of rubble at a packing plant in Florida that received extensive damage. ATF agents are called in from far and wide to investigate such catastrophes.

team traveled from its base in Washington, D.C., to the South Pacific island of Saipan. The reason: to dispose of a huge cache of illegal commercial-grade fireworks smuggled in from China. On this job, the ATF team worked in conjunction with the island's departments of public safety, fire, and public works.

Although fireworks may seem relatively harmless in comparison to a deadly bomb, they are still an enormous threat, in part because they're so common. J. D. Powell, the supervisory explosives enforcement officer with ATF's Explosives Technology Branch, comments,

> These types of explosives devices and fireworks can be extremely dangerous and should never be taken lightly. Over the years more state and local bomb technicians have been injured or killed disposing of illegal fireworks [than with] any other type of disposal operation.

NATIONAL RESPONSE TEAMS

Being an expert in explosives or arson is primarily a field job—that is, you'll spend much of your time at the scene of an incident as well as in a lab or office. The most concentrated form of fieldwork as an ATF employee is likely being a member of what may be the bureau's most elite groups: the National Response Teams (NRTs) and International Response Teams (IRTs).

As a member of one of these elite groups, you'll play an important role in responding quickly and effectively in the wake of a disaster. You'll be assigned to one of four teams stationed around the country. Each of these is self-sufficient and highly mobile, with the ability to have an emergency crew anywhere in the United States within twenty-four hours. Each of these teams typically has thirty to thirty-five agents, specialists, and support personnel. Altogether, as of 2011, the NRT employed a total of about 120 senior special agents and specialists, as well as eighteen laboratory workers and eleven supervisors.

When summoned to a crisis, one team member is designated as the team leader. His or her job, in large part, is to coordinate efforts with local crisis and law enforcement agencies. This is important, since the local agencies will have knowledge that a team from outside the region won't have. So the team makes sure that communication stays open with these other agencies. In the interests of cooperation, the team leader is also careful to avoid assuming complete control of the situation. Mike Bouchard, the now-retired chief of ATF's Arson and Explosives Branch, commented, "ATF doesn't come in and 'take over'. . . from the local incident commander. Our goal is to work with the local authorities."

In addition to the team leader, each unit includes a team supervisor who is responsible for directly managing the group, determining what actions are most needed, and making sure that each member of the team has what's needed over the next few days. (On average, NRT operations last three to four days.)

The rest of the team includes such experts as a fire and explosives investigator, a fire protection engineer, a forensic chemist, a canine team, heavy equipment operators, an evidence technician, an emergency medical technician, and a photographer. These team members are typically experts in more than one field. That is, one member can do the job of at least one other person, depending on the specifics of the situation, and they can switch if needed.

ON THE SCENE

If you're a member of an NRT group, once your team arrives at the scene of a disaster you'll go to work to reconstruct the scene, collect evidence, and identify both the origin and the cause of the disaster. As you and your colleagues progress, you'll meet twice daily: once before the day's work begins and again at the end of the day. These meetings will be key, since they'll give the team members a chance to trade information and ideas while avoiding wasted efforts. In an article in the magazine of the International Association of Fire Chiefs, ATF Special Agent George Lauder wrote,

> The NRT employs a team concept to properly investigate large scenes and deploys team members into two components: one group that processes the scene and one group with a separate investigative-lead element. Working through this model allows both components to maintain constant coordination to ensure investigative continuity.
>
> The NRT has always been successful because it believes that constant communication between the

two elements is necessary. Oftentimes, the scene will dictate the direction of the interviews and vice versa.

Your headquarters during the operation will be a huge truck. These vehicles have been described as "rolling fire investigation toolboxes." Each includes a wide variety of equipment: pop-up shelters, GPS and laboratory instruments, cameras, laptop computers, saws, drills, evidence-collecting equipment, and much more. Some tools are as simple as shovels, toolboxes, and wheelbarrows to clear debris (or heavy excavation equipment, if needed). But they can also be highly sophisticated instruments, such as infrared devices to locate victims who may be under rubble.

Not surprisingly, the trucks also come equipped with various kinds of personal protective gear. This gear includes heavy-duty helmets, gloves, and turnout clothing (like those worn by firefighters), as well as respirators and hazmat (hazardous material) suits. Furthermore, there is space in the trucks where witnesses can be interviewed and shops where equipment can be repaired.

There are very strict rules governing the use of equipment during an operation. For example, a generator in the truck powers any electrical tools used during the cleanup operations. This avoids the possibility that gasoline might leak from them and be mistaken as evidence of an accelerant. Also, team members are careful to inspect and wash their equipment, boots, and clothing after each use. This helps avoid contaminating any evidence the tools might have picked up, and helps

PINPOINTING THE CRIMINALS

Being a criminal profiler is an example of an unusual but important career within the ATF. Profilers use behavioral science to study repetitive, violent crimes by looking at patterns to create psychological profiles of offenders. These profiles, in turn, can yield important investigative clues.

Behavioral profiling is a highly specialized field, one for which very few law enforcement officials are qualified. An ATF profiler is even more specialized than other profilers. In fact, the ATF is the only federal agency that employs a geographic profiler. Geographic profiling focuses on the physical locations of connected crimes. The intent is to find the general area where an unknown offender would be likely to live, which in turn can provide clues to his or her exact location, as well as personality and habits. It's a highly sophisticated version of the low-tech method police once used to see crime patterns: sticking pins in a map.

One instance of an ATF geographic profiler in action occurred in 2010 during the investigation of the East Texas church arsons. The ten burned-out churches were spread out over three counties, but the bureau's profiler was able to help pinpoint where the next fire would most likely occur. Retired ATF agent Larry Smith, who was part of the team investigating those incidents, commented, "I'd say the geographical profiler was pretty dead on with her prediction. We used this information and looked at the areas of the fires. Using that information, the teams were able to begin to focus on major choke points where major roadways came together."

prevent any bits of evidence from being transferred from one part of the crime scene to another.

FORENSIC SCIENTISTS

As an NRT or other investigative team collects physical evidence from a bombing or fire scene, the next phase in the process is the responsibility of forensic scientists. Typically, these experts are based in labs, including the ATF National Laboratory Center (NLC) in Maryland, or in satellite labs in Atlanta and San Francisco.

Sometimes, however, forensics work takes place outdoors. Forensic chemist Michelle Reardon comments, "The analysis work we do here in the lab is crucial, but it's always fun when you can leave your lab coat behind, go out to a crime scene and start digging around in the debris. It's good to get your hands dirty. That's why I joined the National Response Team."

In addition to forensic chemists like Reardon, many other scientists with expertise in certain fields can be involved in the analysis phase of the work. Among these fields are

- DNA and fingerprint analysis of samples from such evidence as debris, confiscated bomb materials, guns, or packaging material used in smuggling

A forensic expert fires a handgun into a Kevlar bullet trap. Bullets fired into this can be retrieved with minimal impact.

- Explosives evidence analysis, such as blasting caps, fuses, timing mechanisms, and radio-controlled components
- Fire evidence analysis of materials such as debris and recovered accelerants, as well as the creation of full-scale fire scenes, and other methods of determining how and why fires occurred
- Firearms and **toolmarks** analysis, which can identify specific weapons and trace their origins (that is, their points of manufacture or sale)

Not all forensic scientists who work for the ATF are directly involved in fire or explosion analysis. For example, the bureau also employs chemists who perform tests on alcohol or tobacco products to check their purity and authenticity. Some ATF scientists also work in the field of questioned documents, which uses a variety of techniques to check the authenticity and validity of documents such as records kept by gun or explosives manufacturers.

In some ways, your work in forensics will be as rigorous as that in any other branch of science. On the other hand, often evidence will be unusual—perhaps a type of explosive trigger or accelerant not seen before by law enforcement. In that case, the job will require a high degree of creativity and imagination to solve the puzzle. As you tackle this complex blend of science and detective work, new challenges will always come your way. Reardon comments, "I like piecing things together. It's interesting to collect all this evidence and then try to figure out what happened."

In addition, sometimes your job as an ATF forensic scientist will involve things other than the immediate analysis of cases. For example, you may need to test new technology or techniques that the ATF is considering adding to its tool chest. You may also work on longer-range projects, such as studies that will advance forensic knowledge and techniques.

INVESTIGATORS AND INTELLIGENCE RESEARCHERS

Forensic scientists for the ATF generally work in labs and therefore have relatively little direct contact with the public or people in the explosives or firearms industry. In contrast to this is a job that does deal often with people: being an investigator. If you become an ATF investigator, your job will send you to a wide variety of places and put you in a wide variety of situations, both in the United States and overseas.

Among your duties will be to interview people and companies in the explosives and firearms industries; consider requests from people who want to work in those industries; and inspect buildings and other facilities for safety compliance. You'll also focus on looking for and identifying evidence of wrongdoing: that is, falsified records, licenses, or inventories.

If you find violations of laws or any suspicious circumstances, you'll report it for further investigation or arrest. Sometimes, you'll be involved in surveillance activities designed to catch offenders. Much of an investigator's job is painstaking, especially since offenders are constantly finding new ways to commit crimes and create false records. On the other hand, the job often generates dramatic results—for example, when teams prove cases against large-scale smuggling and gun-trafficking operations and other criminal activities.

The job of Intelligence Research Specialist (IRS) is not greatly different from an investigator's work. If you become an IRS, you'll focus on gathering, identifying, analyzing, and reporting on information connected to ATF cases. The data can come from such diverse and widespread sources as phone records, confidential informants, or e-mail communications.

Often the cases you'll tackle will be complex affairs that can last for years. For example, you might work

ATF Special Agent Gary Smith remotely operates the Mini Andros II, a bomb-defusing robot.

on cracking large-scale criminal operations such as arson rings (organizations that arrange arson for reasons such as insurance fraud). As the evidence in these cases will be deeply hidden and difficult to sort out, much of your job will go beyond just collecting the data. It'll also be detective work. You'll need to look for patterns and see connections among seemingly unrelated incidents or pieces of evidence.

These cases often cross multiple international or state borders. In your job as an intelligence researcher you'll work closely with law enforcement professionals from a variety of agencies, including local police departments, other federal agencies, your counterparts overseas, and INTERPOL, the international police organization.

PROFESSIONAL AND
SUPPORT PERSONNEL

Only a select few who apply for a job with the ATF will meet all the requirements to be hired in positions such as special agent, investigator, forensic specialist, or intelligence expert. However, there are dozens of other professional and support positions that might be a good fit for you.

Professional and support personnel work mainly behind the scenes, so their day-to-day jobs are different from those of the high-profile special agents. Nonetheless, the bureau couldn't function without them. Lawyers, psychologists, financial officers, administrative staff, and many other professionals are part of this network. Furthermore, there are dozens of other support roles, from surveillance technicians to secretaries and mechanics.

You can view a list of current positions, and get an idea of the work they'll entail, by visiting www.opm.gov/. Some of the job areas you might see include the following:

- Applied science, engineering, and technology (focusing on the "nuts and bolts" of communication, surveillance, and other fields that use high-tech instruments and tools)
- Business management (concentrating on areas such as human resources, security, finance, law, and records management)
- Information technology (building, installing, maintaining, and operating IT operations)

- Investigative surveillance (conducting surveillance operations)
- Other career opportunities, such as graphic arts,
office management and logistics, public affairs, human
resources, budget analysis, secretarial work, administration, accountancy, evidence storage and management, building security, database management, and
maintenance of buildings, weapons, and vehicles
- Photographers (performing a variety of roles in
forensic, surveillance, crime scene documentation,
and research)

Your career with the ATF, no matter what job you take on,
will have one automatic and important benefit. You'll know
that you are helping to protect your country and community
from danger.

On the other hand, personal satisfaction is hardly enough.
No one can live on satisfaction alone. You still need shelter,
food, a budget for leisure activities, and more. So, like any other
large organization or company, the ATF offers its employees a
range of salaries and benefits.

SALARIES AND BENEFITS

PEOPLE WHO WORK FOR FEDERAL AGENCIES ARE generally well paid, and ATF employees are no exception.

Like other federal workers, they receive salary and benefits packages that are set according to general guidelines. For special agents, investigators, and professional staff, this means being paid according to a standardized plan called the General Schedule (GS), or on a variation of this basic plan.

THE GS

The GS has fifteen pay grades. They are called "GS-1," "GS-2," and so on. Within each grade are ten steps. Each grade and each step carries with it a certain salary level. The level you begin at will depend on the specific job you have and on various other factors. For example, your experience and education might put you at a higher level to start with.

As is generally true with salaries in government and the private sector, salaries within the ATF are usually adjusted

An ATF agent takes photographs amid the rubble of the Kinston Fibers textile plant as crews battle a fire.

every year to account for inflation. That is, they rise to reflect changes in the cost of living. To see current pay grades, and to learn more about the General Schedule and the government's policies concerning salaries for federal employees, visit the U.S. Office of Personnel Management's website, specifically the page "Information on Federal Pay and Leave": *www.opm.gov/oca/*.

Moving up the GS ladder depends on several things. For example, one factor is seniority—that is, the number of years you have been on the job. Typically, federal employees start to move up the pay grade scale two or three years after they've completed the probationary period. Other factors that typically affect salary include the complexity of your responsibilities and the difficulty of the work you do. Another factor is the quality of your performance evaluations. These evaluations are "report cards" that judge how well you are doing. Generally, these evaluations are done by one of the senior employees in your department.

If you are a special agent or an investigator, the degree of potential danger you might face is also a factor in your pay. For example, federal law enforcement employees who work in dangerous situations are typically eligible for hazard pay. (Generally, this is a bonus for a onetime assignment, rather than part of a person's regular salary.) Factors such as these are part of a program called Law Enforcement Availability Pay (LEAP), which is designed to compensate employees with hazardous duties for the type of work and any additional (or unusual) work hours that come with it.

Some federal law enforcement officers, including ATF special agents, are paid according to a modified version of the GS. This special schedule is called the GL-LEO (for "law enforcement officer"). A typical new special agent might enter at the GL-5 level. For an employee at that level, the base salary as of 2012 was about $34,000. The base salary of an investigator was between about $27,500 and $41,500. Where you fall within this range will depend on your experience and education.

These salary ranges may seem relatively low, but advancement can be quite fast and will raise your base pay considerably. Furthermore, agents and investigators assigned to regional field offices are eligible for what is called locality pay. This is a percentage of your base salary. Depending on where you are assigned, you might receive locality pay, which is 14 percent to 35 percent of your base salary.

The starting pay grade for professional specialists, such as linguists, IT technicians, forensic scientists, and some other employees, is often at the GS-5 level. As of 2012, the starting salary at this level was $27,431. Meanwhile, the salaries, benefits, and responsibilities for support positions are typically lower than for agents, investigators, and professionals. On the other hand, getting a support staff job is a way to get your foot in the door at the bureau. It is clearly a good starting point for moving on to a more senior position, especially if you can go to school while on the job.

Unlike special agents, investigators, professionals, and many support staff members, **blue-collar** federal employees are usually paid according to a plan called the Federal Wage System (FWS). The Federal Wage System is designed to make sure that government salaries are roughly the same as those in the private (nongovernmental) sector.

Many blue-collar jobs within the ATF are paid on an hourly basis. For example, an automotive mechanic in 2012 could expect to earn about $15.50 an hour to start, depending on the region.

The range of jobs within the ATF is broad, so it's no surprise that the average pay of its employees combined is also broad. In 2012, this average was $65,000. But this is just an average. The individual positions, of course, vary quite a bit. Near the top of the range, for instance, senior special agents in 2012 earned about $100,000 and senior investigators earned about $91,000. Near the bottom of the range, office assistants averaged about $28,000 and human resources assistants about $31,000. In between were such salary points as investigator, $64,000; information technology specialist, $70,000;

intelligence research specialist, $69,000; chemist, $59,000; technical specialist, $63,000; and secretary, $33,000.

BENEFITS

In addition to their salaries, all full-time federal employees are eligible for a wide variety of other benefits. These include life insurance plans, savings plans, reimbursement for travel expenses, and paid days off for national holidays, such as New Year's Day and Independence Day.

Employees are also eligible for annual vacation leave and sick leave days. As is generally true in any work environment, details of paid leave days and other benefits depend on seniority. In the case of special agents, for example, annual leave (vacation time) is earned at the rate of thirteen to twenty-six days per year of employment, with a maximum accumulation of 240 hours per year. Sick leave, meanwhile, is earned at the rate of thirteen days per year of employment and may be added up without limit.

One of the most important benefits for employees and their families is a comprehensive health plan. Depending on the position, ATF employees are eligible for a variety of low-cost health and/or life insurance plans. The ATF also provides extra financial aid and benefits for employees who are injured or disabled while on the job. Similarly, the families of agents who are killed or permanently disabled while on duty are compensated.

In addition, other programs are available for employees who need an extended leave for a reason such as the birth of a child, or the need to recover from a serious illness or care for an ill family member. The ATF follows federal guidelines that

The headquarters of the ATF since 2008.

allow employees to take up to twelve weeks (three months) of unpaid leave in such situations. Another policy in federal law enforcement positions concerns hardship transfers. For example, suppose you and your family need to move to another city to care for an ill or elderly parent. In that case, the bureau will usually try to transfer you to a field office close to where you would like to be.

Meanwhile, federal employees are also covered by a system called a voluntary leave transfer program. Voluntary leave lets ATF employees donate unused annual leave days to other employees who have used all their available days off. Typically, voluntary leave transfer is used when an employee might need extra time to recover from an injury or illness, or to care for a family member.

A further benefit for ATF employees is its Foreign Language Award Program. This program provides cash awards to anyone who is fluent in one or more foreign language(s) and makes significant use of that language (or languages) while on the job.

The ATF also offers its full-time employees various other benefits. For example, you can take advantage of a savings plan to help you invest your money wisely. The bureau also maintains a physical fitness program, which gives employees access to gyms and other facilities.

RETIREMENT

If you stay with the ATF until retirement age, the bureau's retirement and pension plans come into effect. As is true in most businesses and government organizations, the amount of money you'll get after retirement depends on factors such as your salary and how many years of service you've given the bureau. There is no official retirement age for most ATF employees, although special agents are eligible for retirement benefits at fifty and must retire by fifty-seven.

Retirement from the ATF doesn't necessarily mean you'll leave the workforce. After all, many people have no desire to retire at fifty. Many former bureau employees choose instead to take on another career. For example, if you're retiring as a special agent, the skills you've learned, and the experience you've had, guarantee that you will be a valuable commodity on the job market. Many retired special agents go to work for other law enforcement agencies or federal organizations. Still others teach, go into law practice, work with nonprofit organizations, or become private investigators or security consultants.

All in all, the salary and benefits that come with a career in the Bureau of Alcohol, Tobacco, Firearms, and Explosives make working there a very attractive job choice. However, it is clear that there are many more—and better—reasons than money alone to join the team. Interesting, fulfilling, and important work—that's what you'll find with a career with the ATF.

GLOSSARY

accelerants—Chemicals, such as gasoline, that make fires spread faster.

accredited—Officially authorized by a recognized body.

arson—A fire that has been deliberately set.

auditors—Specialists in examining financial records.

ballistics—The scientific study of firearms as they relate to criminal activity.

blue-collar—Term describing positions that typically can be filled by persons lacking a college education; for example, mechanics who keep the ATF's fleet of vehicles in good order.

bootlegging—Participation in the making, distribution, or selling of illegal substances or products.

flammable—Easily ignited and quickly burned.

forensic—Having to do with the law; forensic science is science done in the interests of law enforcement.

incendiary—A substance that sets or creates a fire.

résumé—Also called a curriculum vitae (CV); a summary of a person's education, work experiences, and life experiences, typically for a job application.

revoked—Denied or taken away.

toolmarks—Distinctive marks left by an unusual weapon, such as a screwdriver or wrench.

NOTES

NOTES

INTRODUCTION

pp. 8-9, "[Investigators] try to keep . . .": Patrik Jonsson, "Texas church fires: Who's behind them?" *Christian Science Monitor*, February 10, 2010, www.csmonitor.com USA/2010/0210/Texas-church-fires-Who-s-behind-them.

p. 9, "I think maybe . . .": quoted in Ashley Hayes, "String of church arsons has east Texas residents on edge." *CNN.com*, February 10, 2010, http://articles.cnn.com/2010-02-10/justice/texas.church.fires_1_church-fires-arson-church-web-site?_s=PM:CRIME.

p. 10, "Talk about bold . . .": quoted in Kenneth Dean, "Trail of Terror: Church Arson Investigators Tell Their Stories." *Tyler* (TX) *Morning Telegraph*, February 11, 2011, www.tylerpaper.com/article/20110211/NEWS1201/110219974.

p. 10, "There have been serial arsons . . .": quoted in Layron Livingston, "ATF looking for 3 persons of interest in church arsons." *KLTV.com*, February 12, 2010, www.kltv.com/story/11976780/atf-looking-for-3-persons-of-interest-in-church-arsons?redirected=true.

p. 11, "He just did some things . . .": quoted in Dean, "Trail of Terror."

p. 12, "Learning the results . . .": quoted in Dean, "Trail of Terror."

p. 12, "ATF has been . . .": quoted in "East Texas Arson Task Force Arrests Two." *atf.gov*, www.atf.gov/press/releases/2010/02/022110-dal-task-force-arrests-two.html.

CHAPTER 1

p. 16, "While ATF is primarily concerned . . .": "ATF Explosives Program," *atf.gov*, www.atf.gov/explosives/programs.

p. 16, "As suggested by its name . . .": "The ATF and Its Responsibilities." *TRACATF*, http://trac.syr.edu/tracatf/ atwork/current/atfResponsibilities.html.

p. 17, "It would make explaining . . .": Quoted in "Risk reporter [sic] talks with Mark D. Jones of the ATF." *Church Insurance Risk Reporter*, Fall 2002, www. churchmutual.com/riskreporter/displaycontent. php?id=29&page=qa.

p. 17, "We fashion ourselves . . .": Quoted in Jerry Markon, "FBI, ATF Battle Over Turf." *Erie* (PA) *Times-News*, May 11, 2008, *Goerie.com*, www.goerie.com/apps/pbcs.dll/ article?AID=/20080511/NEWS07/805110404/-1/RSS.

p. 18, "It's not the bureau's . . .": "Industry Operations Investigators," *atf.gov*, www.atf.gov/careers/investigators .

p. 20, "One of the most historical . . . ": "Jesse James gun, effects to be sold during James D. Julia's extraordinary firearms auction Oct. 6-7." *Antiques Trader*, September 18, 2009, www.antiquetrader.com/article/ jesse_james_gun_effects_at_julia_firearms_auction/.

p. 21, "Back then, it was all about booze . . . ": Scott Glover, "Gunning for some fun, skills and insight." *Los Angeles Times*, August 7, 2009, http://articles.latimes.com/2009/ aug/07/local/me-atf7.

p. 25, "Trafficking in contraband cigarettes . . .": "ATF Executes Search Warrants in Contraband Cigarette Trafficking Investigation." *atf.gov*, July 13, 2011, www.atf.gov/press/

releases/2011/07/071311-sea-atf-executes-search-war-rants-in-contraband-cigarette-trafficking-investigation.html.

p. 31, "I was an avid reader . . . ": Tom Cramer, "Forensic Profile: ATF Forensic Chemist Recognized for Outstanding Scientific Achievement." *Forensic Magazine*, October/November 2006.

p. 32, "Any fire investigation . . .": Ed Comeau, "National Response Teams help local agencies investigate fires." *National Fire Protection Association*, May/June 1998, www.efilmgroup.com/News/National-Response-Teams.html.

p. 32, "The ATF brings resources . . . ": Quoted in Ed Comeau, "National Response Teams help local agencies investigate fires."

CHAPTER 2

p. 39, "Although the internships . . . ": The Partnership for Public Service, "Hands-on federal internship: Learning the ropes at ATF." *Washington Post*, August 9, 2010, www.washingtonpost.com/wp-dyn/content/article/2010/08/09/AR2010080903799.html.

p. 42, "It has been very interesting . . . ,": "ATF Internship Tracks Firearms Trafficking," Sam Houston State University, *College of Criminal Justice News*, December 2, 2010, http://shsucj.blogspot.com/2010/12/atf-internship-tracks-firearms.html.

p. 50, "The job of . . . ": "ATF Pre-employment Physical Task Test." *atf.gov*, www.atf.gov/careers/special-agents/physical-task-test.html.

CHAPTER 3

p. 57, "The goal . . . ": "Risk reporter [sic] talks with Mark D. Jones of the ATF." *Church Insurance Risk Reporter,* Fall 2002, www.churchmutual.com/riskreporter/displaycontent.php?id=29&page=qa.

p. 57, "When this exceptional . . . ": "Accelerant and Explosives Detection Canines." *atf.gov,* www.atf.gov/explosives/programs/explosives-detection-canines.

p. 58, "The fundamentals . . . ": "Bombs Away: Getting a Unique Education at the Hazardous Devices School." *fbi.gov,* www.fbi.gov/news/stories/2004/december/hds122004.

p. 61, "These types . . . ": "ATF to conduct large scale disposal of illegal explosives." *Saipan Tribune,* April 5, 2010, www.saipantribune.com/newsstory.aspx?newsID=98500.

p. 62, "ATF doesn't come . . . ": Quoted in Ed Comeau, "National Response Teams help local agencies investigate fires." *National Fire Protection Association,* May/June 1998, www.efilmgroup.com/News/National-Response-Teams.html.

p. 63, "The NRT employs . . . ": George H. Lauder, "On the Front Line with the ATF National Response Team," *IAFC On Scene,* International Association of Fire Chiefs, December 2010, www.iafc.org/Operations/LegacyArticle-Detail.cfm?ItemNumber=4127.

p. 65, "I'd say the geographical . . .": quoted in Kenneth Dean, "Trail of Terror: Church Arson Investigators Tell Their Stories." *Tyler* (TX). *Morning Telegraph,* Janu-

ary 13, 2012, www.tylerpaper.com/article/20110211/
NEWS1201/110219974/-1/NEWS12.

p. 66, "The analysis work . . . ": quoted in Tom Cramer,
"Forensic Profile: ATF Forensic Chemist Recognized for
Outstanding Scientific Achievement." *Forensic Magazine*,
October/November 2006, www.forensicmag.com/article/
forensic-profile-atf-forensic-chemist-recognized-out-
standing-scientific-achievement.

p. 67, "I like . . . ": quoted in Cramer, "Forensic Profile."

FURTHER INFORMATION

BOOKS

Dunn, John M. *Prohibition*. Farmington Hills, MI: Lucent, 2010.

Hoffman, Dennis E. *Scarface Al and the Crime Crusaders: Chicago's Private War Against Capone*. Carbondale: Southern Illinois University Press, 2010.

Newton, Michael. *Bomb Squad*. New York: Chelsea House, 2010.

Newton, Michael. *Crime Fighting and Crime Prevention*. New York: Chelsea House, 2010.

WEBSITES

Bureau of Alcohol, Tobacco, Firearms, and Explosives
www.atf.gov

Exploring Program
http://exploring.learningforlife.org/services/
career-exploring/law-enforcement

National Integrated Ballistic Information Network
www.nibin.gov

USAJobs
www.usajobs.gov

BIBLIOGRAPHY

BOOKS

Damp, Dennis V. *The Book of U.S. Government Jobs.* McKees Rocks, PA: Bookhaven, 2011.

Queen, William. *Armed and Dangerous: The Hunt for One of America's Most Wanted Criminals.* New York: Random House, 2007.

Queen, William. *Under and Alone: The True Story of the Undercover Agent Who Infiltrated America's Most Violent Outlaw Motorcycle Gang.* New York: Random House, 2005.

Vizzard, William J. *In the Cross Fire: A Political History of the Bureau of Alcohol, Tobacco, and Firearms.* Boulder, CO: Lynne Rienner, 1997.

PERIODICALS/WEBSITES

"Accelerant and Explosives Detection Canines." *atf.gov*, www.atf.gov/explosives/programs/explosives-detection-canines.

"The ATF and Its Responsibilities." *TRACATF*, http://trac.syr.edu/tracatf/atwork/current/atfResponsibilities.html.

"ATF Executes Search Warrants in Contraband Cigarette Trafficking Investigation." *atf.gov*, July 13, 2011, www.atf.gov/press/releases/2011/07/071311-sea-atf-executes-search-warrants-in-contraband-cigarette-trafficking-investigation.html.

"ATF Explosives Program," *atf.gov*, www.atf.gov/explosives/

programs.

ATF Internship Tracks Firearms Trafficking." Sam Houston State University, *College of Criminal Justice News*, December 2, 2010, http://shsucj.blogspot.com/2010/12/atf-internship-tracks-firearms.html.

"ATF Pre-employment Physical Task Test." *atf.gov*, www.atf.gov/careers/special-agents/physical-task-test.html.

"ATF to conduct large scale disposal of illegal explosives." *Saipan Tribune*, April 5, 2010, www.saipantribune.com/newsstory.aspx?newsID=98500.

"Bombs Away: Getting a Unique Education at the Hazardous Devices School." *fbi.gov*, www.fbi.gov/news/stories/2004/december/hds122004.

Comeau, Ed, "National Response Teams help local agencies investigate fires." *National Fire Protection Association*, May/June 1998, www.efilmgroup.com/News/National-Response-Teams.html.

Cramer, Tom, "Forensic Profile: ATF Forensic Chemist Recognized for Outstanding Scientific Achievement." *Forensic Magazine*, October/November 2006, www.forensicmag.com/article/forensic-profile-atf-forensic-chemist-recognized-outstanding-scientific-achievement.

Dean, Kenneth, "Trail of Terror: Church Arson Investigators Tell Their Stories." *Tyler* (TX) *Morning Telegraph*, February 11, 2011, www.tylerpaper.com/article/20110211/NEWS1201/110219974.

"East Texas Arson Task Force Arrests Two." *atf.gov*, www.atf.gov/press/releases/2010/02/022110-dal-task-force-arrests-two.html.

"Eliot Ness," *Biography.com*, www.biography.com/articles/ Eliot-Ness-9542066.

Glover, Scott, "Gunning for Some Fun, Skills and Insight." *Los Angeles Times*, August 7, 2009, http://articles.latimes. com/2009/aug/07/local/me-atf7.

Hayes, Ashley, "String of Church Arsons Has East Texas Residents on Edge." *CNN.com*, February 10, 2010, http://articles.cnn.com/2010-02-10/justice/texas. church.fires_1_church-fires-arson-church-web-site?_ s=PM:CRIME.

History of ATF—1789–1998, *atf.gov*, www.atf.gov/about/ history/atf-from-1789-1998.html.

Jonsson, Patrik, "Texas Church Fires: Who's Behind Them?" *Christian Science Monitor*, February 10, 2010, www.csmonitor.com/USA/2010/0210/ Texas-church-fires-Who-s-behind-them.

Lauder, George H., "On the Front Line with the ATF National Response Team." *IAFC On Scene,* International Association of Fire Chiefs, December 2010, www.iafc.org/ Operations/LegacyArticleDetail.cfm?ItemNumber=4127.

Livingston, Layron, "ATF Looking For 3 Persons of Interest in Church Arsons." *KLTV.com*, February 12, 2010, www.kltv. com/story/11976780/atf-looking-for-3-persons-of-interest-in-church-arsons?redirected=true.

Markon, Jerry, "FBI, ATF Battle for Control of Cases." *Wash-*

ington Post, May 10, 2008, www.washingtonpost.com/
wp-dyn/content/article/2008/05/09/AR2008050903096.
html.

The Partnership for Public Service, "Hands-on federal
internship: Learning the ropes at ATF." *Washington Post*,
August 9, 2010, www.washingtonpost.com/wp-dyn/con-
tent/article/2010/08/09/AR2010080903799.html.

"Risk reporter [sic] talks with Mark D. Jones of the ATF."
Church Insurance Risk Reporter, Fall 2002,
www.churchmutual.com/riskreporter/displaycontent.
php?id=29&page=qa.

Salary Table 2011-GS, www.opm.gov/oca/11tables/html/
gs.asp.

INDEX

ABOUT THE AUTHOR

ADAM WOOG is the author of many books for adults, young adults, and children. His most recent books are *Military Might and Global Intervention* in the Controversy! series, and the five other titles in this series. Woog lives in his hometown of Seattle, Washington, with his wife. Their daughter, a college student, is majoring in criminal justice and criminology.